In the Woods

Written by Akimi Gibson
Illustrated by Jon Goodell

SCHOLASTIC INC.

New York   Toronto   London   Auckland   Sydney
Mexico City   New Delhi   Hong Kong   Buenos Aires

What can you see?

I can see a tree.

I can see the bee!

I can see a log.

I can see the frog!

I can see you and me!

Text copyright © 2002 by Scholastic Inc.
Illustrations copyright © 2002 by Jon Goodell.
All rights reserved. Published by Scholastic Inc.
Printed in the U.S.A.

ISBN 0-439-45556-1

4 5 6 7 8 9 10   23   11 10 09 08 07 06 05 04 03